Life Coaching Guide

*How to Be A Life Coach &
Launch A Life Coaching Business
In Less Than 30 Days*

Sara Stephens

Table of Contents

Introduction

So you're either curious about life coaching, want to expand your life coaching knowledge, or want to begin a profitable career as a life coach. I'm excited to tell you that all of your questions regarding life coaching will soon be answered!

Life coaching is one of the most rewarding careers. As a professional life Coach, you will help people to new perspectives; achieve more balance between work, family and social life; bring people to a softer level of enjoyment with life by being more in the present moment; and motivating people to get into action to achieve goals that I've been put off for *way* too long.

The demand for life coaching keeps growing each year, as we are trying to make better livings for ourselves and our families while keeping a level of balance within our lives. Sometimes life can feel like a glass faucet, and as the water keeps getting more and more full, it can feel overwhelming as the water begins to pour out of the glass. This is one of the many areas where a life coach is needed.

Let's first take a look at what a life coach is, and how it all got started so that you can familiarize yourself with its roots!

Chapter 1
Getting Started – Life Coaching 101

What is a life coach?

The first question that most people tend to ask when it comes to life coaching is – What is a life coach?

While athletes have a coach to help them in the game so they can perform to the best of their ability, some of us have a life coach that helps us with life and motivates us to do our personal best in areas like family, relationship or work.

A life coach is a person who supports a client and empowers him (or her) so that he can achieve his goals, dreams, and objectives in life. Life coaches specialize in various areas such as career, health, education, dating, and personal growth. A client can consult with a life coach if he has problems with his job, relationships, health, or business.

The coach acts as a mentor. Her job is to see to it that you succeed and fulfill your wants in life. She does this by engaging a client in deep meaningful conversations, asking her powerful questions and helping her know his goals, what she wants in life, and how to achieve all of it.

In life coaching, the client is the boss. Coaches only guide their clients or 'coachees' to help themselves achieve whatever they want. A life coach does not interfere with a client's personal life but gives her client the power to maintain total control of her life by helping her understand herself, her goals, and how she sees the world.

History

The profession of 'life coaching' first came about in the early 80's as an extension of business and sports coaching. It was first created by American psychologist Michael Brown.

Coaching was used in the world of professional sports. Trainers of athletes and champions found that through helping athletes recognize and achieve their goal, self-believing and positivity, athletes harness their natural talent and become winners in their field. It went beyond training and fitness, coaches learned to help athletes in other aspects of their life such as their relationship with friends and family, financial concerns, and even religious and spiritual journeys.

From sports, coaching came to influence the world's top companies. Companies started to teach communication techniques and management. It was a form of training to executives so they can reach their best potential and improve their performance at work. Politicians and government officials have also started to try hiring a coach so they can make best decisions in work. After the media has taken on the phenomena with reality TV shows - life coaching became one of the raves of the general public.

Life coaching is a new profession, but many professionals and historians argue that life coaching may have been done back in the time of Socrates or even much earlier. Socrates was a man who opened his disciples' minds through asking questions, and humans have always had this innate hunger for knowledge, progress, understanding and enlightenment that can be traced back as far as the beginning of civilization.

Nowadays, life coaching is gaining popularity. Many people seek a life coach because they want to look forward, act focused, and enjoy life as best they can.

The sessions

Life coaching is highly confidential- a client can speak freely about private matters to his coach. There has to be an established trust between the client and his coach for the sessions to work effectively.

During a life coaching session, a life coach engages their clients in question-and-answer exercises that promote self-understanding and self-growth. The clients have the option to pick which area he wants to start the coaching first. And from that the coach can move from area to area as he interviews the client.

Coaching is different from psychotherapy since it involves not much prying about people's pasts. Life coaching focuses on the *now,* it is present oriented. A coach may briefly ask questions about a client's past but would primarily focus on his present self.

If you want to learn more about the how to be in the present moment for yourself and your clients, I highly recommended one of my colleagues books How To Live In The Present Moment, where he goes into detail and provides steps to accessing the present moment.

Life coaches will identify a client's strengths and weaknesses along with the skills he needs to improve. After an initial assessment, the coach will tell the client her analysis of the clients' skills and from there, she will encourage the client to set a goal. Coaches can offer suggestions of skill improvements for her client. She will explain to the client the benefits of developing his skills and the fruitful results after the goal is attained, while remaining impartial to whether or not the client takes the suggestion.

Coaching sessions last 30 minutes to an hour and can be over the phone, online (Skype), or face-to-face, depending on what works best for both of you. Coaches use different tools during initial sessions. They may use visuals or verbal presentation to stimulate the interest of their client.

When it comes to salary, beginner life coaches usually charge $100- $200 per session, while experienced life coaches charge fees from $250 to as high as $750. Life coaches usually earn a higher income compared to advisors and counselors.

Is life coaching a career for you?

If you love helping people and are compassionate, empathetic, and wise, then life coaching can be a living for you.

Life coaches are normally those people who we always run to for advice and guidance. Their words do not just heal; they uplift spirits, bring joy and help people make better decisions.

Some life coaches have been through terrible experiences and want to help people who are undergoing the same troubles. These people are willing to share important life lessons so others can learn from them and avoid going through the same pitfalls.

Life coaching does not only prove to be satisfying for the client but also to the coach. It is a two-way learning process, an ideal partnership that you and your client get to experience - you learn from your clients as they learn from you.

Many life coaches would take pride in the joy that comes from their work. Seeing their clients transform and achieve their goals is the best reward they could have. A successful and happy client by the end of the session means a job well done!

Chapter 2
Skills, Abilities and Qualities of a Successful Life Coach

Being a life coach requires certain skills, abilities, and qualities that are essential for you to properly mentor your clients and establish a successful coaching career. It goes beyond your ability to motivate and inspire people. Your skills are your strength, and these are the ones that are evaluated when you work with your clients.

1. Ability to empower and motivate

A life coach encourages his clients to feel excited, and happy about what they are doing, and where they are at in life. Success comes to those who enjoy their work, to those who are empowered and not oppressed, and those who have a feeling of freedom to make choices. Often times, clients will come to you because they feel "stuck" in a situation. It is your job to keep your client motivated to work towards her goal. If your client lacks the motivation then she will surely fail – you will both fail.

Here are a few examples of questions you might ask:

- How would it feel to wake up every morning and know exactly what your day will look like?

- Who is someone that you admire or look up to? How would it feel to be in his/her shoes?

- If you could do anything with your life right now, what would you do?

These are just a few examples of the thousands of questions out there that you can ask.

Ability to give appropriate feedback

A life coach should know how to respond properly and give his client appropriate feedback. Be friendly and supportive when giving your client feedback. Compliment him and never get angry or belittle your client. A client will respond positively if you know how to give importance to her and make her feel valuable. She will then be more open to your guidance. When giving negative feedback, choose words that are suitable and would not sound disrespectful. Your feedback should never be judgmental or condescending because it will demotivate the client.

Communication skills

As a life coach you are expected to have superb communication skills. Wherever you may be contacting your client – on the phone, computer or face-to-face, you should be able to reach out to your client and send him clear, concise messages. You must also respond correctly and understand the messages she is sending you. If you happen to miss something that the client said or didn't understand him, then be open with your client and let him know. Life coaches should be great conversationalists and good listeners.

If you want to improve your conversational or storytelling abilities, I recommend The Conversation Method by Matt Morris, in which he explains steps and strategies for telling a story as well as how to easily start a conversation with anyone.

Confidence

A life coach should exude an aura of confidence but not arrogance. Confidence is a sense of knowing who you are - your strengths, your weaknesses, things that excite you, as well as things that make you uncomfortable, and a willingness to admit them all to yourself. That is the essence of being confident with whom you are as an individual.

Your clients will often be people who have low self-esteem, self-worth, and those that are often unsure about how they will work out life. It is your duty as their life coach to help them find confidence within themselves, a quality you must first possess.

Creativity

If you love your work and you are passionate about helping people, creativity comes rather easily. One of the best ways to access creativity, is to clear your mind of all external thoughts and stresses. It often helps to meditate for a few minutes before coaching sessions.

Accessing creativity is necessary as a life coach because it is important to come up with creative ways to help a client access his or her creativity, which is done by asking open-ended questions that resonate with your client. In addition, creativity is often accessed through the body, not the head. Therefore ask the client to pay attention to her body and ask the client what her body is telling her.

Empathy

Be compassionate and understanding. Let your client know that you care and are set on helping him because you understand how he feels. Use this as an opportunity to put yourself in the clients' shoes and really try to feel how he feels.

With life coaching, it is important to understand that you don't have all the answers, and it is not your responsibility to tell the client what to do. Instead, your responsibility is to ask the client questions for him to access and discover his own answers. People would much rather discover answers by themselves, as opposed to being told what to do.

Your job is to understand and empathize with him. Make him feel that you are worthy to be trusted. Empathy will help you win his trust.

Honesty

Be honest with your client even if he is not honest with you. Avoid making insincere or tasteless comments because if you're being dishonest your tone of voice will give you away, just as his or her tone of voice will help you determine if he's being honest with you.

Knowledge

A life coach should be well researched in his field. What good are you to your client, if he knows more about the issue at hand than you yourself? Change is constant, you have to adapt to it. Update and research about the changes in the different areas of self –development or your area of expertise.

Choose an area your area passionate about whether it's dating coaching, family coaching, or personal- development coaching – be sure you are knowledgeable about it and enjoy the subject. Pursue your love of learning and make it your goal to learn more about your job with every client you take. As the saying goes, there is something new to learn each and everyday.

Listening Skills

Listening and hearing are two different things. Hearing is a physical body process. The ears do the work and the brain translates it for a person. Listening on the other hand is an interpretative process. It involves understanding, interpretation and attention.

When we listen to another person, we provide our time and effort. It is key give to give your full attention, listen to your client, and simply be with your client so that it feels like you are meshing together. He will believe in your commitment to help him.

Another skill of listening, which often takes time to develop, is to use and listen to your intuition. Intuition usually is like a glimpse of light in your mind that will only last a few seconds. But, when you offer it (or just blurt it out) to your client it will offer new ways for both of you to access more creativity and greater learning.

Observation skills

As a life coach you should be able to read your client through careful observation. You should be keen to her verbal and non-verbal behavior. Studying your client's behavior will shed some light to his personality and how he perceives you. By studying nonverbal behavior you can discern if your client is experiencing discomfort with what you are telling him.

Organizational skills

Confusion and problems arise when there is no effective organization. As a coach you should be organized, your client will see organization as professionalism. The more professional you handle your client, the more he is likely to recommend you to his friends, which is the greatest and easiest source of marketing!

Patience, a good-natured tolerance

Some clients will give you a hard time. You will need all the patience you can get to be able to do your job right. When you lose your temper, or make a haughty remark, your client will regard you as unprofessional and will no longer trust what you say.

Positivity

A positive outlook in life can be contagious. As a life coach you should practice what you preach. Approach your clients in this attitude and they will reciprocate. Life coaches should always maintain a positive tone and writing when dealing with their clients.

Positivity is a skill that can be developed. In a sense it is transforming your negative thoughts into positive ones, and many people say that positivity is a step above positive thinking because it is at the core of who a person has become.

One of my colleagues created a book based on Positive Thinking and how to completely transform your negative thoughts to positive ones, which I highly recommend.

Time Conscious

Life coaches should be punctual. You should show your client that you are a respectful, trustworthy individual that he can count on. When you cannot be on time for some reason, be sure to contact your client and apologize for it. Building trust starts with the way you treat him.

Questioning skills

A life coach does not give the client answers to his questions; instead he helps him find his own answer and guides him to take subsequent measures to help solve his problem. A good coach asks powerful questions.

A person can grow as an individual only if they discover the answers to their problems by themselves. There are also instances when a coach becomes an advisor and a teacher. In every advice you make to your client, be sure that he is asking for it, that he granted you permission first to give him advice.

Chapter 3
Coaching Tools and Technique:
Coaching Models

A life coach's main goal is to help his client do his best. A brilliant coach can help a client in decision making, solving problems, learning skills, and progressing on their careers.

There are trainings for coaching available in online courses and there are also schools for coaching. Reading this book will help you develop your coaching skill, and give you some helpful techniques to become a great coach.

Coaching Models

Here are some powerful models and technique for helping you structure your coaching sessions.

The Personal Brilliance Model

The Personal Brilliance Model is a philosophy. It is a way of life. This model helps one look at how they are living each and every day of life. It explores key aspects of life, which influence your views of yourself and the world.

There are seven elements of the Personal Brilliance Model:

1. Desire – A coach supports a client's wants and desires. He helps them identify and define their dreams. Some clients already know their desires and as a coach your job is to support him to make this desire a reality. Other clients are still confused of what they really desire, during this instances – it is a coach's job to help clients discover their dreams.

2. Believe – It is important for a client to believe in his dreams. As a life coach you must help your clients to recognize the beauty and possibility of their dreams.

3. Achieve - The fastest way to achieve is to take action. A coach helps his client determine the action that he has to take when working towards his goals. During occasions when things go out of plan, it is a coach's job to bring their clients back on track and achieve what they have planned to do.

4. Permission – Permitting you to achieve is a key element in success. There are clients who may feel that their goals are too big, or beyond their potential. A coach may ask a client if there is anything that holds him back to achieve his dreams. The coach teaches him then to permit himself to achieve regardless of anything that he thinks is an obstacle.

5. Commitment – Failure after the first try is not a reason to give up. Clients may fail and as a coach you should help and encourage them have a strong commitment to their goals. In this process, you may have to inform your client of the threats and challenges he will have to face. As a life coach, you will work with him to develop a strategy for addressing these obstacles. What does he need to stay committed?

6. Acknowledgement – Your efforts and each small success towards a goal is a reason to celebrate. You must learn to acknowledge them and recognize them for the client's hard work.

7. Choice – The secret to being personally brilliant is to always make conscious choices in your life. Let your

client know this. Teach him that success depends on how much you know about what you want and what you don't want. It is your duty to help him make the right choices in his life and to get clear on his decisions.

For more information on setting goals, I highly recommend this book written by life coach Matt Morris titled, <u>Goal Setting: 10 Easy Steps To Keep Motivated & Master Your Personal goals.</u>

Your Best Life Coach Process

The Your Best Life Coach process is another coaching tool coaches use to get the best outcome from the sessions with their client. This coaching tool helps the client through a journey of self-discovery while preparing her to the changes he will have to do with his life to reach his goals.

The Your Best Life Coach Process consists of three parts:

1st step – Know where you are

2nd step – Know what (or who) you need to be

3rd step – And do it!

The client is encouraged to do each step with the help of his coach as a guide. If the client does not have answers for himself, the coach will help him discover and support him to work towards his goal.

The GROW Model

GROW stands for Goal, Reality, Options and Wrap up. It is a model consisted of a four-step structure, which uses basic elements for an effective connection with a client during the coaching session.

Goal – Visualize the desired outcome by discussing areas chosen by the client himself.

Reality – Question your clients to help them comprehend clearly the reality of the situation.

Options – List all the options and identify the best solution to achieving your goals.

Wrap Up- Plan steps and identify possible obstacles. Follow up every day as you work towards your goals.

For more information, take a look at a wonderful coaching model titled, Co-Active Coaching by Karen Kimsey-House.

Chapter 4
Coaching Tools and Technique II: Questions and Exercises

A life coach will help her client discover what she values most in life, her best abilities for him to understand himself. These are things that get the person excited about life. It's also a way to take an outside perspective to see how the client spends most of her time.

Self-understanding will lead to internal harmony and peace. If a client does not know herself well enough, she may fail in achieving her goals because she doesn't know what she *really* wants in life. Included in this chapter are different coaching questions and exercises that professional life coaches often use in their sessions.

The 10 Questions to Discover What Moves You

1. What 3 things do you value most about yourself?

2. What 3 things do you want most in your life?

3. What are 3 things you that make you happy?

4. What 3 things do you think are important to you with regard to your family?

5. What 3 things are important to you as a parent/student/friend /employee?

6. What 3 things do you appreciate most about your friends?

7. What 3 things do you desire most in a partner/spouse?

8. What 3 things do you value most about your career or work?

9. What 3 things do you love to do for recreation?

10. What 3 things do you value most about your spirituality?

And if you want a client to expand on a topic, say either "What else?" or "Tell me more." This usually gets the client to open up more for more self-exploration.

The 11 Questions to Find Your Best Self

1. What did you like to do as a child?

2. What sense did you live your life by? Did you see things? Did you talk a lot about yourself? Are you more sensitive to sounds? Did you love to feel things? Describe.

3. What are your greatest achievements?

4. What are your skills, abilities, talents that shine out in you?

5. What things do you have passion for?

6. What do you like most about yourself?

7. What three positive adjectives would you describe yourself?

8. What are your most cherished memories of being you? What are your most memorable memories of having fun?

9. What do you know to be true about you when you are at your best? What word would suit you when you are at your best?

10. What is a metaphor to describe your life right now?

11. What is your life purpose?

3 Questions to Clarify Your Outcomes

1. What are the things grateful for in your life right now? List as many as you can.

2. What are the things you don't want but you have in your life right now? List as many as you can.

3. What are the things you want but you don't have in your life right now? List as many as you can.

The Wheel of Life

The wheel of life is a tool that gives clients a visual representation of their life as it is now and ideally how it will be in the near future.

With the help of the wheel, your client will be able to consider which part of their life is off balance- which part they are giving too much focus and which part they are neglecting.

How to Perform the Exercise:

1. Draw a circle and add 8 spokes to it. The circle will represent the wheel of life and the spokes are the important things you value in life.

2. You can label your spokes with: relationship, family, career, social life, self improvement, health, fun, money

3. Draw a line on each spoke and label it between 1 and 10, 1 being the worst and 10 being the best. Ask these questions to your client:

- How happy are you in this part of your life?

- In a scale of 1-10, how would you rate this area of your life?

4. Add up his score and ask powerful questions to your client. Example:

- Have you ever scored higher than the number you recorded?

- Can you tell what it was like or how it felt when you were higher up the scale?

- What was happening in your life when you were higher up the scale?

- Have you ever scored lower than the number you recorded? How did that feel?

- What things did you do to move up the scale?

- Did you learn something when you were lower on the scale?

- What number on the scale do you want to be?

- What kinds of actions are you willing to take to move up the scale?

- If you move up the scale, how will you know it?

- What action must you do to move higher by one point on the scale by next week?

- What things can block you from moving up the wheel?

- How can you prepare for these obstacles - how can you overcome them?

5. After discussing the wheel of life and asking the client these questions. Let him record his future goals.

The Daily Diary

A daily diary is the easiest way a client can keep track of her improvement. Furthermore, diaries serve as an outlet of feelings that may be hard to express verbally. A coach can encourage his client to maintain a daily diary.

Many people are so busy they forget to acknowledge what they have achieved for the day. It can be hard to commit to a diary. A diary is solely for your eyes only. You should maintain to write daily and keep it safe away from the eyes of other people. At least once a month, re-read and self-reflect on all your entries from the previous month and notice how much you have improved.

Building Confidence

Most clients experience work problems and a troubled life because they are afraid to do things. They lack confidence and are scared of the unknown. It is one of a life coach's jobs to help clients with their self-development, self-growth and self-esteem.

Client Exercise:

1. Think of a time in your life when you felt really confident. What are you confident at? How does confidence feel to you?

2. When you are hesitant about something, remember the feeling of confidence, and you will start to feel confident. Think about this confident feeling.

3. Imagine yourself seeing your confident form as a color. What color would it be?

4. Does your confidence feel hot or cold? Double the temperature of this confident feeling.

5. In what direction do you feel it spinning? Spin it faster and faster.

6. How much more confident do you feel now?

Time to Dream

Some people find it hard to visualize their goals because they don't take time to dream. This may be caused by their busy schedule or stressful work routines. Let your client know the importance of relaxation and dreaming.

Make a schedule for your client to find some alone time, free from any distractions, music, people, or conversations. Encourage your client to think about his dreams before actually listing it down on paper. This is a helpful strategy for the client to get clear on what he wants in life.

Chapter 5
Effective Marketing Ideas
for your Coaching Service

Coaching has attracted many professionals in its field. Given these facts, one might think that life coaches are earning fortunes enough to attract many white-collar workers in the field. Unfortunately, this is not true. Many starting coaches struggle to find clients and earn enough money for themselves.

A successful practice requires not just skill and knowledge but a good marketing technique. Here are six easy steps to become successful in your coaching practice.

Know your strategy and work on it

In coaching, before you start getting clients and helping them with their life problems, you must first plan a strategy and a good organized system.

- Know whom you are going to work for. Who is your target audience?

- How will you deal with problems in work and what could be potential problems?

- What coaching models or training exercise should you be using to solve the problems of your clients?

- How can you create a marketing message that will attract people to call out their problems and ask my help to show them a solution based on their own goals and values?

Use low-cost and practical ways first to get clients

You don't have to spend a fortune to attract your clients. Start small and improve your tactics step by step as you go along.

- Ask for referrals. Referrals from your previous trained clients. The people you have worked with will be willing to refer you to clients, especially if you've helped them greatly.

- Do online marketing. Sell your services with a web promotion plan with an attractive web design and good development strategy.

- Build alliances and work on relevant organizations and associations.

- Ask for past clients to post recommendations to your website or for Yelp, Google, or Yahoo reviews. This is a good way to get new potential clients.

- Always have a free 30-minute sample session so that the potential client can feel the value of life coaching, and be more willing to sign up for more sessions; and always ask for the person if they want to become a client. If you don't ask, nothing will happen.

Make smart deals

A lot of coaches settle for a low pay for their services when they can actually raise their salaries and earn the price they want by making smart deals with their clients. When you make deals with your client, you have to be open and honest. You should consider both your client's side and yours and try to see what prices will work best for both of you.

Handle objections wisely and do not argue with your client. If you know how to make smart deals, business will develop naturally and easily.

Are you a trainer? For a double pay, you can offer both coaching and training services. You can offer training, coaching or a combination of both. Making deals and raising your price will be easy if you offer both services.

Serve your clients well enough to keep them for life

The best source of revenue comes from your current clients. Give unqualified importance to your clients and find ways to help them in every aspect of their life – each of the areas from the Wheel of Life. You must be sensitive to the needs of your client, so as you can suggest further what needs to be improved in his life. You can offer your services to other people in his circle, like his family or co-worker.

Establish a firm and see that your hard earned money is spent well

Firm building makes it possible for you to earn more revenues. As a coach, you know the importance of developing strategies and methodologies and the values of intellectual property. Use this advantage to create additional programs and product services that you can offer to the market. Sell tools to help your clients and improve your services. You can try books, information products, membership programs, seminars, etc. Know how to connect with other coaches and build a good team with good deals and engagements.

Take action and create your dream business

It is necessary to take time to plan and review all your strategies and ideas. You should remember to make marketing and firm building your top priorities. With your successful coaching and commitment to your business, you will attract clients, make more revenue and establish a bigger firm. Get started and build the business of your dreams!

One of my colleagues, Daniel Robbins wrote an eBook titled "Be A Powerful Life Coach: The Secret To More Clients, More Coaching, and More Wealth", which is filled with excellent marketing strategies to get started and build your career as a life coach.

Chapter 6
A Guide to Smart Management of Time, Energy and Effort as You Start Your Life Coaching Business

Life coaching is a rewarding profession. Whether it's the passion, the money or the spiritual fulfillment that drives you to work, life coaching makes your own life meaningful. You are able to experience the happiness that comes from the success of the people you have helped- you are certainly contributing and making a difference!

But then the life of a coach isn't for everyone. Coaching requires hard work, and a lot of your time, energy and effort. Don't be deceived, coaching might look easy like tutoring or counseling but if you work with many clients- there is a tendency for you to mix them up and get confused.

Here comes time, energy and effort management to help you survive through the day. Work stress can be managed and here's how.

Time, Effort and Energy Management

Many people think that the reason they are unable to do more work is because they don't have more time. The truth is, it isn't only the quantity of time that matters, the quality of time and how you spend it too should be considered.

Here are some tips that can help you manage your time more efficiently, especially if you are beginning your career as a life coach:

- *Make a list of your priorities for each day.* This avoids you from doing little unnecessary tasks that get people side tracked, distracted or unfocused.

- *Create a to*-do-list. Break down activities, and settle deadlines so you can work efficiently without forgetting something.

- *Do the most important task of the day first!* It is easy to start with the most important task. Do the works that has deadlines first before starting on another project.

- *Shut the door, turn off emails.* If you have a hard time focusing and getting all your work done on time, try minimizing distractions.

- *Time track.* Keep a time log for a week and see how much time you are spending on unimportant activities. Track which time you get the most interruptions, as well as the time of day that you are most productive. This will make it easier to manage your time and avoid distractions.

- *Clean up the clutter.* Some people find it hard to focus if they work in a messy desk. By clearing up and organizing your things, your mind will clear out clouding clutters that make you unfocused too.

- *Know what to do with your Spare Time.* Use your spare time to relieve stress or prepare for busier tasks by starting with small tasks - For example, taking time to refresh after a stressful coaching session, or preparing for the next coaching session.

- *Pick your time carefully.* When are you most focused? Early morning, late in the afternoon, or during the night? The key to get things done efficiently is to schedule the most challenging work to the time when you are most energized and alert.

- *Avoid Overload.* Don't forget to include time for rest, relaxation, leisure, eating, exercise and socializing for your schedule. Take short breaks during work.

- *Don't put off everything until the last minute.* Most of us are guilty of doing this. Doing things in the last minute only results in low quality work. Schedule your time and do your work well ahead.

- *Get enough sleep and exercise.* It is important to take care of your health. Many have done great success in their work but have neglected their health as a result of working long hours without rest. Balance your life and maintain a healthy well-being.

Following these work management tips will not only give you extra hours in a day but it can also improve the quality of your work and quality of your life. We do not know the true value of time until we have lost it. Time is gold. Time is life. Time is relentless.

Conclusion

By the end of the day, it will still be perseverance and passion that will make you a successful life coach. It is all about helping other people. Life coaching has its perks along with its downsides. By reading this book, you have equipped yourself with helpful information to be successful in the field.

Thank you for reading this. May you have the best of luck in your future endeavors.

- Sara Stephens

Other Recommended Books

1.

How To Live In The Present Moment: Let Go Of The Past & Stop Worrying About The Future

2.

How To Be A Powerful Life Coach: The Secret To More Clients, More Coaching, and More Wealth

3.

The Power of NLP - Attract More Wealth, Better Health, And Improve Relationships

4.

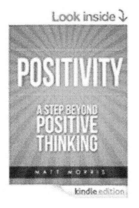

Positivity: A Step Beyond Positive Thinking

5.

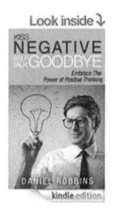

Kiss Negative Self-Talk Goodbye: Embrace The Power of Positive Thinking

6.

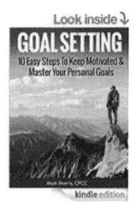

Goal Setting: 10 Easy Steps To Keep Motivated & Master Your Personal Goals

7.

<u>Emotional Intelligence: Understand Emotional Intelligence To Improve Self Management and Increase Your Social Skills</u>

8.

<u>Emotional Intelligence: The Genius Guide To Maximizing Your Emotional Intelligence - Master Your Emotions, Thoughts, and Communication Skills</u>

Made in the USA
Las Vegas, NV
12 March 2022

45495781R00022